THE BASICS BOOK

of X.25 Packet Switching

SECOND EDITION

Motorola Codex

**MOTOROLA
UNIVERSITY
PRESS**

ADDISON-WESLEY PUBLISHING COMPANY, INC.
Reading, Massachusetts · Menlo Park, California · New York
Don Mills, Ontario · Wokingham, England · Amsterdam
Bonn · Paris · Milan · Madrid · Sydney
Singapore · Tokyo · Seoul · Taipei
Mexico City · San Juan

The publisher offers discounts on this book when ordered in quantity for special sales. For more information please contact:

Corporate & Professional Publishing Group
Addison-Wesley Publishing Company
Route 128
Reading, Massachusetts 01867

ISBN: 0-201-56369-X

1 2 3 4 5 6 7 8 9 10   MW   9594939291

First printing, November, 1991

MOTOROLA UNIVERSITY PRESS

The Motorola Codex Basics Book Series
The Basics Book of Information Networking
The Basics Book of X.25 Packet Switching
The Basics Book of ISDN
The Basics Book of OSI and Network Management
The Basics Book of Frame Relaying

WORLD HEADQUARTERS
20 Cabot Boulevard
Mansfield, Massachusetts USA 02048-1193
Tel: (508) 261-4000, Fax: (508) 337-8004

SELECTED WORLDWIDE LOCATIONS
Belgium:
SA Motorola NV, Brussels
Tel: 32 (2) 718-5411
Canada:
Motorola Information Systems, Brampton, Ontario
Tel: (416) 507-7200
France:
Motorola Codex Systemes D'Information, Paris
Tel: 33(1) 4664-1680
Germany:
Motorola GMBH, Darmstadt
Tel: 49 (6151) 8807-0
Hong Kong:
Motorola Asia Ltd., Causeway Bay
Tel: 852 887-8335
Ireland:
Motorola Codex, Dublin
Tel: 353 (1) 426-711
Israel:
Motorola Israel Information Systems Ltd., Tel-Aviv
Tel: 972 (3) 751-8333
Japan:
Nippon Motorola Ltd., Tokyo
Tel: 81 (3) 3440-3311
Spain:
Motorola Codex Spain, Madrid
Tel: 34 (1) 634-0384
Sweden:
Motorola AB Codex Datacommunications Sector, Stockholm
Tel: 46 (8) 795-9980
United Kingdom:
Motorola Codex, Wallington
Tel: 44 (81) 669-4343
United States:
Eastern Area, Clifton, NJ Tel: (201) 470-9001
Southern Area, Dallas, TX Tel: (214) 690-5221
Central Area, Schaumburg, IL Tel: (708) 576-2036
Western Area, Long Beach, CA Tel: (310) 421-0086

PREFACE

This is one in a series of booklets designed to explain in everyday language some of the basics of data communications networks. At Motorola Codex, we aren't limited to any one networking approach, and we don't believe you should be either. Together these bookets are intended to help you understand more fully the variety of approaches available. (If you feel the need to brush up on basic basics, ask for a copy of our *Basics Book of Information Networking.*)

We hope you find *The Basics Book of X.25 Packet Switching* a useful tool as you continue to explore cost-effective ways to make your network more productive. Should the book prompt further questions about the benefits or implementation of an X.25 network, we'll be happy to help you find the answers.

TABLE OF CONTENTS

INTRODUCTION

This book falls into three broad sections. The first, comprising two chapters, describes **how** packet switching works: Chapter 1 looks at all the necessary network components, while Chapter 2 describes network operation.

The second section, consisting entirely of Chapter 3, tells **why** packet switching works. It covers the X.25 standard that makes packet switching networks possible.

The third section, comprising three chapters, looks at **when** and **where** packet switching is both applicable and beneficial. Chapter 4 considers some of the more pertinent applications. Chapter 5 focuses more specifically on benefits. Chapter 6 delves into some specialized environments.

Please feel free to dip into the book at whatever point you feel most comfortable. We realize some of you will be more familiar with the subject than others. Some will be more "how" oriented, some more "why," and some more "when and where." But whatever your questions about packet switching, our aim is to help you find useful answers. At the end of the book you'll also find out more about our credentials, as well as how to talk to us one-on-one.

WHY ALL THE INTEREST IN PACKET NETWORKS?

If you're reading this book, you're clearly already interested in the possibility of building a packet switched data network (PSDN), or you've heard enough about the subject to want to know more. In either case, it might be useful to review briefly some of the reasons for the growing interest in packet switching.

In recent years, the growth of distributed networks and the drive toward data communications standards have made packet switching an increasingly attractive networking solution. Why? Because packet switching offers greater connectivity, sharing of host resources and transmission facilities among many users, standardized network access, independence from single-vendor proprietary solutions, interfaces to public data networks, and sophisticated network control and management.

X.25 has emerged as the dominant, internationally endorsed data communications standard for connecting terminals and computers to packet switching networks. Today both large and small network users who have a widely dispersed population of terminals and who require a high degree of connectivity are turning to X.25 solutions.

(Note: throughout the remainder of this book, we'll be using "X.25" and "packet switching" interchangeably. Technically a distinction does exist—we'll cover it in Chapter 3. However, common usage has made these terms virtually synonymous. Since most people think of them that way, we decided to use them that way.)

WHAT IS PACKET SWITCHING?

Now for the obligatory definition: packet switching is a data networking technology in which user data is segmented into small units (packets) and transmitted from the sending user to the receiving user over shared communications channels (see Figure 1). Each data packet carries additional information that allows the network to route that packet from one user to another accurately and reliably. The size of the packet of user data is limited to some maximum number

In a packet switched data network (PSDN), information is segmented into small units, or packets, and transmitted over shared communications channels.

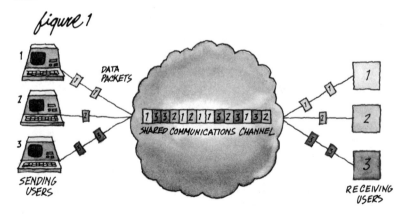

figure 1

SENDING
USERS

DATA
PACKETS

SHARED COMMUNICATIONS CHANNEL

RECEIVING
USERS

of characters. These are measured in 8-bit bytes called **octets**. User messages in excess of that maximum length are broken up into multiple packets that follow one another, in order, through the network from the sender to the receiver.

WHAT IS A VIRTUAL CIRCUIT?

Packet switching differs from circuit switching in that it uses what are called **virtual circuits**. The circuit is called "virtual" because:

- it is made up of bandwidth allocated on demand from a pool of shared circuits
- there is no direct physical connection between two parties exchanging data over a packet network
- the connection is instead a logical one

The "logic", that is, the routing and destination information, accompanies each packet through the network. For all these reasons, packet networks are often referred to as **connectionless** networks.

The difference between a packet switched network and a circuit switched network (regular telephone lines) is outlined in Table 1. The primary advantage to packet switching is cost. Because packet network resources are shared among many network users, packet switching is less expensive for many applications than a dedicated circuit (more on benefits in Chapter 5).

THE INTERACTIVE NATURE OF PACKET NETWORKS

Packet networks are best characterized as real-time, interactive networks. In other words, applications that tend to benefit from a packet network approach are ones in which:

- users are geographically dispersed
- a human-to-host computer interaction takes place
- data must be exchanged in both directions in real time
- data delivery must be reliable and accurate
- the volume of data in both directions is relatively small
- the gaps between transmissions are longer than the transmissions themselves, resulting in low line utilization

Although Table 1 shows that packet networks impose a small transport delay between communicating users, the delay is usually so short as to be unnoticeable by a terminal operator or insignificant when compared to host-computer application processing delays.

PUBLIC, PRIVATE, AND HYBRID PACKET NETWORKS

There are three kinds of packet networks: public, private, and hybrid (a combination of the first two). Which one is appropriate for you depends on your applications and your bandwidth needs.

Many large organizations—such as those in the transportation, banking, finance, and insurance industries as well as state and federal government—have data transport requirements that justify their having private data networks. There are some very good reasons for building a private X.25 data network. For example, it reduces transmission costs by allowing multiple applications to share the same transmission media. It also cuts central site hardware costs by providing a single-line interface to front-end processors and host computers. And it provides the added benefit of both standards support and integration into public networks as well as easy migration to future offerings such as ISDN. In fact, most large packet switching networks are really hybrids, combining public and private transport services. (More on these private packet networks in Chapter 6, where we'll also consider how businesses choose between statistical multiplexing and packet switching.)

We'll take a closer look at packet switching applications in Chapter 4 and benefits in Chapter 5. But now it's on to **how** packet switching works, starting with network components and architecture.

TABLE 1: A COMPARISON OF CIRCUIT AND PACKET SWITCHING

CIRCUIT SWITCHING	PACKET SWITCHING
Suitable for Voice and Data Communication	Suitable for Data Communication Only (at present)
End-to-End Terminal Compatibility Required	Speed, Code and Protocol Conversion Done by Network
Subject to Blocking (Busy Signal)	Virtually Non-Blocking
Long Call Set-up Delay (Seconds)	Short Call Set-up Delay (Milliseconds)
Transparent to User Data Streams	Network Compatibility to User Data Required
Virtually No Transport Delay	Short (Millisecond) Network-Imposed Transport Delay
Moderately Accurate (1 in 10^6 Packet Errors)	Highly Accurate (1 in 10^9 Packet Errors)
No "Overhead" Information Required	Some "Overhead" Information Required (about 6%)
Inefficient Use of Network Resources	Efficient Use of Network Resources
Flat Rate (Usage Insensitive) Pricing*	Usage Sensitive Pricing*
Distance Sensitive Pricing*	Distance Insensitive Pricing*

*Applies to public PSDNs only.

1

PACKET SWITCHING NETWORK COMPONENTS

OR

my PAD or yours

A packet switched data network (PSDN) has five major components:

- local access components (LAC)
- packet assemblers/disassemblers (PAD)
- packet switching nodes (PN)
- network links (NL)
- a network management system (NMS)

Figure 2 shows a schematic diagram of a PSDN with each of the major components labeled. The characteristics, functions, and interrelationships of these components are discussed below.

LOCAL ACCESS COMPONENTS

To transmit data through a PSDN, the data must first move from the end-user to a packet assembler/disassembler (PAD) or to a packet switching node with a built-in PAD function. There are three local access components needed to accomplish this purpose:

- an end-user data terminal
- a local access facility (physical line)
- an end-user transmission device (modem)

A packet switched data network consists of five major groups of components.

(Note: Some end-user equipment is capable of packetizing data; these devices do not need a PAD to access the network.)

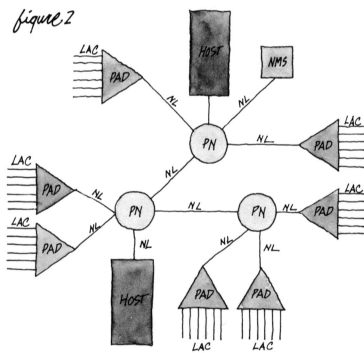

figure 2

LEGEND - PN: PACKET SWITCHING NODE   PAD: PACKET ASSEMBLER/DISASSEMBLER
NMS: NETWORK MANAGEMENT SYSTEM   LAC: LOCAL ACCESS COMPONENT
NL: NETWORK LINK

The three types of local access lines commonly used for packet switching today are:

- switched analog lines (i.e., dial-up)
- leased analog channels (i.e., private lines)
- leased digital channels (i.e., DDS circuits)

The type of local access line and the desired speed of operation determine which transmission technology is used to reach the network. (For more detailed information on local access lines and devices, see Codex's *Basics Book of Data Communications*.)

PACKET ASSEMBLERS/DISASSEMBLERS

A packet assembler/disassembler (PAD) allows the user to access the network. **The PAD's primary function is to ensure compatibility between the various user devices (hosts and terminals) and the packet switched network.** Terminal devices vary by manufacturer, communications protocol employed, speed of operation, and code employed.

However, regardless of the terminal used, the output must be standardized before it is transported to the packet switching node. The PAD performs this function by "packetizing" data from inbound terminal devices. This packetized data (in a standard format and complete with overhead information) is now sent to the packet switching node for routing. **The Codex 6505 Asynchronous PAD channels non-X.25 data streams into X.25 packet networks.** (PADs connect to switching nodes via access ports or gateways.) Conversely, a PAD may be used to depacketize or disassemble the data prior to sending it to the destination host or responding user terminal.

Other functions performed by the PAD may include:

- physical line concentration
- call setup and clearing functions
- protocol conversion (see Chapter 3)
- code conversion
- protocol emulation (see Chapter 6)
- local switching functions
- local call recording (billing) functions

PADs are designed for less throughput than switching nodes (in the range of 10-100 packets per second, or roughly 10,000-100,000 bits of data). Sometimes the PAD function is incorporated in the switching node; similarly, some PADs may perform switching of packetized data.

Note: The term PAD as used here and throughout this book refers to equipment used to connect *asynchronous* devices to the PSDN. Other protocols require specialized PADs.

The Codex 6500 Series is a high-performance family of packet data networking products.

PACKET SWITCHING NODES

At the heart of a packet switching network is the packet switching node (PN). **Its most important function is to ensure that each packet is routed to its proper destination.** Other functions include:

- call record journalling (billing)
- internal network diagnostics
- support of direct host computer access
- inter-network gateway connections

Often, to assure maximum availability, packet switching nodes are installed in a redundant configuration. In other words, two critical components are duplicated to provide backup for each other.

Packet switching nodes are high throughput devices. The current generation of switching nodes will support throughputs of 70-3000 packets per second; the next generation will increase that figure tenfold in the next few years.

The Codex Modulus® Series of space-saving enclosures houses a broad range of X.25 and other networking devices.

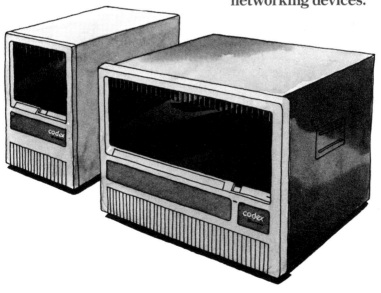

5

NETWORK LINKS

The physical circuits that connect packet switching nodes to each other are called network links (NLs). Many different transmission technologies can be employed in network linking, including:

- analog circuits
- digital circuits
- microwave systems
- satellite systems

By far the most common network link technologies in use today are:

- Digital Dataphone service, and other similar services offered by the interexchange carriers (in the U.S.) or the Public or Postal Telephone and Telegraph Companies (PTTs) around the world
- point-to-point analog private lines

Network link speeds can vary from 9.6 Kbps to 56/64 Kbps. High speed circuits are most common; these will increase toward T1 speeds in coming years.

Figure 1 shows that only "packetized" data is transported by the NLs to and from packet switching nodes. Because the NLs form the framework of the switching network, they are referred to as the **backbone packet network** or the **backbone layer**. The PADs and their associated local access components are often referred to as the **access network** or **access layer**.

This architectural distinction between access data (varied speed, codes and protocols) and backbone data (common protocol and format with network overhead) is important in the design and smooth operation of a packet switched data network.

NETWORK MANAGEMENT SYSTEM

The network management system (NMS) is responsible for the control and monitoring of the packet switched network.

The most critical function of the NMS is storage and maintenance of the network database. This database is the master copy of all the software and configurations resident in each network node. In the database, the NMS contains routing tables and end-user interface profiles. In case of network problems, the appropriate database records can be down-line loaded through the NLs to a malfunctioning node to correct the problem without dispatching a field technician. By performing such functions through the NMS, the network nodes can operate in **unattended** mode, thereby reducing network operating costs dramatically.

Other network management system functions include:

- access security checking/call setup assistance
- collection of operational statistics from the network nodes
- receipt of alarms from malfunctioning network components
- collection and storage of billing data from the network nodes
- performance of network diagnostic tests
- performance of corrective actions to remedy network functions remotely

The NMS console terminal or workstation provides an interface between a human operator and the network management computer. From the workstation, the network operator can perform a wide variety of functions such as:

- configuring end-user network interfaces
- initiating software or configuration down-line loads
- initiating network diagnostic tests
- receiving trouble reports (alarms) from the packet network
- receiving the results of specific diagnostic tests moments after their completion

The Codex 9300 and 9800 Integrated Network Management Systems perform functions ranging from storage and maintenance of the network database to corrective action to remedy network problems.

To ensure maximum availability in large, multi-technology networks, critical components are duplicated and distributed throughout the network. So much for network components; now let's see what happens when we put them together.

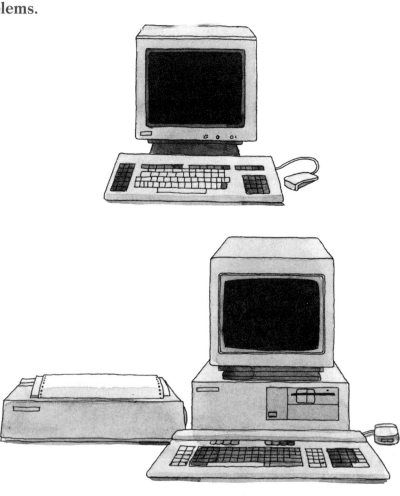

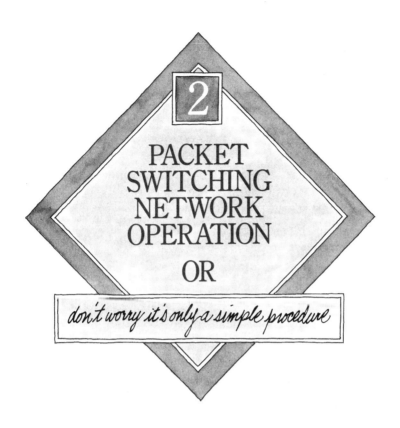

PACKET SWITCHING NETWORK OPERATION

OR

don't worry it's only a simple procedure

Packet switching network operation is really quite simple, but let's take it step by step anyway. (We don't call this a "basics book" for nothing. If this first part seems too basic, you might want to skip a few paragraphs and proceed to the section of this chapter on routing.) Placing a call across a packet switching network is analagous to placing a voice telephone call. The call has:

- an originating party
- a receiving party
- and a specific process by which the call is connected

A successfully completed call establishes a virtual circuit (remember that?) between the two end users. A call through a packet switching network is referred to as a **virtual connection**.

9

THE THREE PHASES OF A VIRTUAL CONNECTION

The three phases of a virtual connection are:

- call setup
- data transfer
- call clearing

During the **call setup phase**, the originator must establish a connection with an access node (PAD) in his or her geographic area by:

- dialing the node's local telephone number in switched access arrangements
- or by powering up the data terminal in leased access arrangements

Once connected to the PAD (a network log-on may be required), the originating user enters the packet network address (see Chapter 3; X.121) of the desired receiving end user (this "address" is similar to a telephone number). If configured, the network will send a successful call-establishment indicator to the originating party after a short period of time (i.e., 100 milliseconds—2 seconds).

In the data transfer phase, the network is transparent to the end users, who perceive that they are physically connected.

The virtual connection now enters the **data transfer phase.** In this phase, the two end users are in communication with each other. They can exchange data in real time in full-duplex mode.

In the data transfer phase, the network is transparent to the end users, who perceive that they are physically connected. They have no indication that the connection is "virtual," or that complex processing is occurring within the network (e.g., packetization/ depacketization, logical routing, code conversion, and speed conversion).

When the transaction between the two users concludes, either may request that the call be disconnected. At that time, the virtual connection enters the **call clearing phase.** Both end users receive an indication that they are no longer connected to each other. In some networks, an indication of the amount billed for the call is returned to the billed party. Either end user is now free to place another virtual call through the network simply by requesting connection to another network address. (Note, however, that once a *dial-up* user terminates a PAD connection by hanging up the phone, he or she must redial before placing further packet network calls.)

ROUTING IN PACKET SWITCHING NETWORKS

In a circuit switched network, there's only one way to get from here to there. In a packet switched network, there are several. The network nodes, under the control of the network database, decide which of these possible routes the packetized data should take. In other words, **routing determines the proper sequence of PNs and NLs necessary to support the virtual circuit required by the originating caller.**

To protect against the failure of key backbone network elements, packet switching nodes are usually interconnected in a mesh configuration. In this configuration, shown in Figure 3, alternate routes may be selected to connect any two users. In the figure, possible routes between User A and User B include:

- NL1; PN2; NL3; PN3; NL5 (primary route)
- NL1; PN2; NL7; PN1; NL8; PN3; NL5 (secondary route)
- NL2; PN2; NL9; PN4; NL4; PN1; NL8; PN3; NL6 (tertiary route)

When key network components are deployed in a redundant or "mesh" configuration, alternate routes are selected transparently to the users.

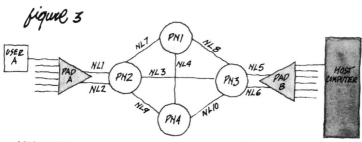

figure 3

LEGEND – PN: PACKET SWITCHING NODE   PAD: PACKET ASSEMBLERS/DISASSEMBLERS   NL: NETWORK LINK

At call setup, the switching nodes translate the receiving user's network address into a virtual circuit route composed of a number of node-to-node hops. Normally, the primary route chosen is the most efficient interconnect path between the end users. When there is heavy traffic or failure along the primary route, the switching nodes may choose a secondary or tertiary route. **All routing occurs transparent to the users**.

Note that in today's packet switching networks, once a particular routing sequence has been selected for a virtual connection, it is maintained for the duration of the call. Packets travel in sequence along that route until the call is cleared.

Figure 3 also illustrates that NLs may be deployed in a redundant configuration, just like PNs. For example, NL1 and NL2 in Figure 3 both interconnect PAD A to PN2. Therefore, a meshed packet switching network using redundant nodes and trunks offers availability far exceeding other data communications methods (e.g., standard dial-up networks or leased line networks).

RESOURCE MANAGEMENT IN PACKET SWITCHING NETWORKS

As with any network, a packet switching network is an organized collection of finite data communications resources. These resources fall into three broad categories:

- **Nodal processing power** (the capacity of the node to process each packet's overhead information and to make decisions based on its content)
- **Nodal buffer capacity** (the capacity of the node to store end user data during overhead processing)
- **Internodal trunk bandwidth** (determined predominantly by the speed of the trunks)

The network must manage these limited resources to ensure low-delay, non-blocking network operation.

To support each virtual connection, a portion of the total network capacity is pre-allocated at call setup time. Therefore, a virtual connection is essentially an "advance reservation" for a certain amount of network capacity in each of the three categories listed above. As a packet switching network grows (more users, heavier traffic volumes), its resources may become depleted. To the end user, such depletion appears as:

- lengthening call setup time
- increasing data transport delays (longer response times)
- complete blocking of end user access

Before such resource shortages become noticeable, the NMC (through its ongoing surveillance of the network) indicates potential critical areas of depletion. Then the network operator may provide additional nodal capacity or trunk bandwidth to maintain the network in an optimal operating state.

ACKNOWLEDGMENT AND ERROR CONTROL
One of the big advantages of packet switching is that it offers **approximately a thousandfold increase in accuracy over typical dedicated analog transmission lines** (dial-up or leased). How is this possible? How are errors prevented in a packet switching network?

To understand the process of error correction, it helps to remember first that a packet in transit traverses the network in a series of hops from node to node via the NLs. More accurately, a packet in transit between two nodes is copied from one node (the origin) to the next (the destination) via the NLs. Immediately after receipt by the destination node, two copies of the same packet exist in the network: the copy received by the destination node and a duplicate still stored in the originating node. Thus the originator can resubmit the data if an error occurs.

That's the short answer. For those who'd like more detail about error detection as well as correction, there follows an expanded version. Each time a packet is copied from one node to another, the destination node processes its overhead information. This process includes a mathematical check (see Chapter 3 for more detail) to determine whether any data corruption (or errors, in common parlance) occurred during its transmission.

A packet in transit between two nodes is copied from one node to the next.

If the destination node finds the contents of the packet to be accurate, it sends a signal back to the originating node. The originating node then erases its copy of the packet. Conversely, if a packet of data is found to be corrupted at the destination node, this node sends a signal back to the originating node to "retransmit" its copy of the packet. The packet is actually "recopied" until the originator receives an indication that an error-free copy of the packet has been received.

The indicators that are sent from the destination node back to the originating node are called **acknowledgments**. Obviously, there are two varieties:

- **Positive acknowledgment (ACK)** = packet received without errors (causes originator to erase duplicate copy)
- **Negative acknowledgment (NAK)** = corrupted packet received (causes originator to retransmit its copy)

DELAY IN PACKET SWITCHING NETWORKS
During a virtual connection, each switching node along the path of the virtual circuit is in constant contact with its upstream and downstream neighbors to ensure the accuracy and reliability of the connection. Packet switching networks can even be thought of as "living" entities because they dynamically adapt to changes in their internal and external environments. But the same intelligent and complex software processes that occur at all times with the network also account for the phenomenon of delay. Two types of delay may occur:

- processing delay
- transmission delay

Packet switching networks can be thought of as "living" entities because they dynamically change with changes in their environments.

Transmission delay results from the time taken by a packet to traverse an internodal trunk between two network nodes. This delay is governed by both trunk line speed and packet size.

Processing delay is the time taken by a given node to process and act upon the overhead information. This delay is governed by:

- the throughput capacity of the particular packet switching equipment deployed and is to that extent vendor-dependent
- the current internal state of the network (i.e., the degree of congestion at any given time).

In addition, the total delay imposed by the network for any one virtual circuit depends on the number of hops along its route. Generally speaking, a circuit with fewer hops exhibits fewer delays than a circuit with more hops. (This is not always true: clearly more hops are preferable when noise or some other problem is obstructing traffic along the shorter route.) The only practical way to be sure of the total network imposed delay between two end users is to take measurements at various times and average the results.

3

PACKET
SWITCHING
PROTOCOLS
OR

a polite introduction to X.25

This chapter is for those who like to understand the principles behind a process. We've seen *how* a packet switching network works; here we look at *why* it works. Which brings us back to the X.25 protocol. You'll recall that in the Introduction, we suggested most people think of "packet switching" and "X.25" as essentially interchangeable terms. How did this come about? Why do most people think of a networking protocol (X.25) as synonymous with a networking technology (packet switching)? In the answer lies one of the chief attractions of packet switching: standardized network access; that is, independence from single-vendor proprietary solutions. But that's getting ahead of our story.

WHAT IS A PROTOCOL?

First a bit of history. (Don't worry, it's only a teeny bit.) Back in the 1960s, when operator terminals were first remotely located from mainframe host computers, data communications protocols became essential. From their remote sites, these terminals usually gained access to the host through a telephone company-provided line. To communicate effectively, the activities of the terminal and the host had to be organized and coordinated in some fashion. Hence the need for **a set of rules and procedures that coordinates and streamlines the flow of information between two communications facility users**—in other words, a **protocol**.

Protocols support many critical communications functions, including:

- establishing a network connection
- routing communications in switched networks
- establishing and maintaining "talker/listener" relationships
- polling in multipoint networks
- controlling errors and controlling flow
- clearing a network connection

THE ROLE OF THE CCITT

Before the mid-1970s, protocol design was in the hands of mainframe host computer manufacturers, who also typically manufactured the operator terminals. Thus a number of different data communications protocols were introduced, each associated with a particular manufacturer, with the result that—well, we all remember what happened at Babel.

Meanwhile, both circuit and packet switched data networks were being offered in Europe and Canada, and public data networks such as Tymnet and Telenet were emerging in the U.S. To avoid the potential chaos of incompatibility among host computers, operator terminals, and data networks—all using different protocols— standards had to be adopted by both manufacturers and data network providers. For packet switched data networks (PSDNs), the present worldwide standards for interconnection are delineated in a series of documents called the **X Recommendations**.

These recommendations are the product of a standardization body known as the CCITT, the Comité Consultatif International de Télégraphie et Téléphonie. The CCITT, a direct descendant of the United Nations, represents a number of UN countries. Every four years the CCITT meets in plenary session to ratify recommendations pertinent to international telephony and telegraphy—or, for our purposes, data communications.

In 1976, the CCITT ratified Recommendation X.25, which specifies a set of three protocols for connecting terminals and computers to packet switching networks. X.25 (and related Recommendations X.3, X.28, X.29, X.32, X.75, X.96, and X.121) form the basis for present-day packet switching.

Note: Because of the coexistence and interconnection of public and private packet switching networks, private network equipment adheres to the same CCITT standards.

WHAT IS X.25?

CCITT Recommendation X.25 is officially entitled "Interface between Data Terminal Equipment (DTE) and Data Circuit Terminating Equipment (DCE) for Terminals Operating in the Packet Mode and Connected to Public Data Networks by Dedicated Circuit."

Perhaps a picture will help. Figure 4 depicts the relationships between DTE and DCE equipment schematically. Although X.25 is often used on network links between packet network nodes, it does not necessarily apply to the protocol used *within* a network. X.25 merely specifies the interface between a data terminal (packet mode DTE) and a packet network node (DCE) for access to a public or private packet network over dedicated lines.

A diagram definition of CCITT Recommendation X.25.

figure 4

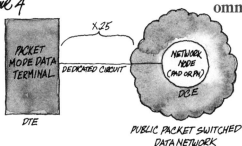

PACKET MODE DATA TERMINAL — DEDICATED CIRCUIT — X.25 — NETWORK NODE (PAD OR PN) — DCE

DTE

PUBLIC PACKET SWITCHED DATA NETWORK

X.25: CONFORMING TO THE OSI REFERENCE MODEL

The remainder of this chapter is for those who like their theory as thick as a seven-layer cake. We won't spend time analyzing the ingredients of all of the layers, only those three that contain abundant portions of our X.25 protocol. First, though, let's pause to admire the presentation of the finished product.

For some years the International Standards Organization (ISO) has been constructing a model that describes the interconnection of data processing systems. This model, known as the Standard Reference Model for Open Systems Interconnection, or the **OSI model**, specifies the characteristics of an open system. Foremost among these is that **overall processes such as error control and call routing are subdivided into seven functional layers.** Each layer is responsible for performing specific processing tasks. The interface between each layer is standardized so that hardware and software systems can be compatible with each other, regardless of their manufacturer. Figure 5 shows the classic representation of two connected open systems, each with seven layers of functionality (according to the OSI model). The open systems shown in Figure 5 could be end-user data terminals or host computers.

The OSI Reference Model subdivides overall data communications processes into seven functional layers.

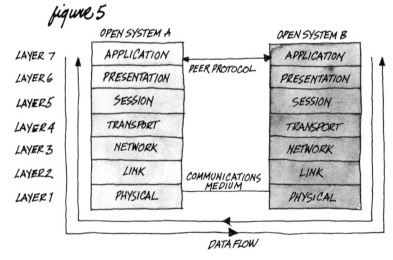

figure 5

	OPEN SYSTEM A		OPEN SYSTEM B
LAYER 7	APPLICATION	PEER PROTOCOL	APPLICATION
LAYER 6	PRESENTATION		PRESENTATION
LAYER 5	SESSION		SESSION
LAYER 4	TRANSPORT		TRANSPORT
LAYER 3	NETWORK		NETWORK
LAYER 2	LINK	COMMUNICATIONS MEDIUM	LINK
LAYER 1	PHYSICAL		PHYSICAL

DATA FLOW

The exchange of overhead information from one open system to the other is through peer protocols between equal layers (layer 4 in one system to layer 4 in the other). The flow of user application data, however, is through adjuncts in the same system (layer 4 in one system to layer 3 in the same system). For example, an automatic teller machine (ATM) transaction can be tracked through a multi-layer system. One application layer provides a direct interface to the person attempting a transaction while the other application layer interfaces with ATM applications software in the bank's host computer. The application layers communicate through peer protocols, performing such transaction-related tasks as debiting an account, dispensing currency, or crediting an account. Actual data flow between the two open systems (the ATM and the host computer), however, is from top to bottom in one system (from the host computer to the ATM), across the communications line, and then from bottom to top in the other system (from the ATM to the host computer). Each time applications data passes downward from one layer to the next in the same sytem, overhead information is added. When that information is removed and processed by the peer layer in the other system, it causes various tasks (error correction, flow control, code conversion, encryption/decryption) to be performed.

That's just a taste of OSI theory. If you find a taste to be as good as a feast, you'll be relieved to recall that a detailed discussion of each of the seven OSI layers and their function is well beyond the scope of this text. (If you *are* interested, check out CCITT Recommendation X.200.)

However, an understanding of the OSI model is helpful for understanding X.25. **The three peer protocols defined in X.25 correspond to the lowest three levels of the OSI model.** Figure 6 shows this correspondence. The OSI model relegates transmission and networking tasks to those three layers, each of which is discussed in the following sections—for those of you whose appetites are now whetted.

LAYER 1. THE PHYSICAL LAYER STANDARD: X.21BIS/EIA232C

The physical layer peer protocol manages the transmission of bits across the physical connection. A physical layer protocol specifies the electrical, mechanical, and procedural aspects of that communication. Layer 1 protocols commonly define:

- the interface connector type
- the voltage levels on the signal leads
- the lead names and their functions
- the procedures by which the signal leads are used to manage bit transport across the communications medium

CCITT Recommendation X.25 specifies a physical layer protocol called X.21 for layer 1 support in PSDNs. X.21 is an 8-wire synchronous interface that is used commonly on circuit switched data networks in Europe. The X.21 interface is not widely used in North America. To accommodate North American needs, the CCITT specifies an alternative physical layer standard called X.21bis. X.21bis is known in the United States as EIA232C (or perhaps more commonly as RS232C).

The EIA232C interface, a standard specified by the Electronic Industries Association (EIA), is widely

The three peer protocols of CCITT Recommendation X.25 correspond to the lowest three levels of the OSI Model.

supported by all manufacturers of data communications equipment in the North American marketplace. (The particulars of the EIA232C interface are specified in the EIA232C document published by the EIA.) The essential point in the

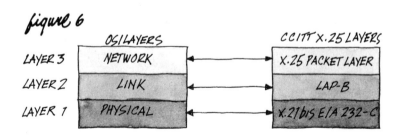

figure 6

	OSI LAYERS		CCITT X.25 LAYERS
LAYER 3	NETWORK	↔	X.25 PACKET LAYER
LAYER 2	LINK	↔	LAP-B
LAYER 1	PHYSICAL	↔	X.21 bis EIA 232-C

current context is that **any device that is EIA232C-compatible is compatible with an X.25 PSDN at layer 1.**

LAYER 2. THE LINK LAYER STANDARD: LAP-B

The task of the link layer peer protocol is to manage the transfer of data units called **frames** from one open system to another. You'll remember that the open systems at either end of the link are a DTE and a DCE. The link layer peer protocol specified in X.25 is called LAP-B (an acronym for Link Access Procedure-Balanced), and the units of data transferred between a pair of layer 2 peer entities are called LAP-B frames.

The LAP-B frame format is shown in Figure 7. Note that the frame is divided into a header area, a user area, and a trailer area. The header and trailer are further subdivided into fields (flag, address, control, frame check sequence). Each of these fields contains a bit pattern that is generated by the sender of the frame, and that is read by the receiver of the frame to perform the functions of the link layer protocol.

The major functions of LAP-B are:

• link management
• error control
• flow control
• failure recovery

Link management. In X.25, LAP-B makes use of several different frame types. Some frames contain end-user applications data. Others are transmitted across the

The LAP-B protocol ensures that data reaching the end user is accurate.

Figure 7

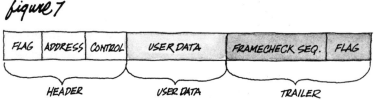

| FLAG | ADDRESS | CONTROL | USER DATA | FRAMECHECK SEQ. | FLAG |

HEADER   USER DATA   TRAILER

link to perform such management functions as accepting or rejecting data frames, disconnecting the link, and setting various link response modes. These frames are commands and responses that coordinate the activities of the layer 2 peer entities in maintaining the link.

Error control. The LAP-B protocol ensures that data is transferred across the link accurately. The sender sequentially numbers each frame sent (in the control field) and fills the frame check sequence (FCS) field with a 16-bit binary number that is mathematically calculated from the contents of the frame. When the receiver gets the frame, it performs the same calculation and compares the result to the number in the FCS field. If the data was corrupted as it passed across the communications line, the receiver signals the sender (using a link management frame) to resend the bad frame, which can be identified by its sequence number. Correctly received frames are acknowledged by the receiver using one form of link management frame. Using this technique to do error detection and correction, the LAP-B protocol provides a high degree of accuracy in its transport task.

Flow control. Flow control refers to the process by which a data receiver signals the sender to temporarily stop sending because of storage or display limitations. Sometimes referred to as throttling, flow control is accomplished by the LAP-B protocol using the frame sequence number and a link variable called **window size**. Window size is the number of frames that can be sent across a link before the sender must stop sending and wait for an acknowledgment from the receiver. If the receiver senses that its memory space is filling up, it simply does not send an acknowledgment until memory space is made available for new incoming frames. In addition, the receiver can use a specific type of link management frame to signal the sender that it is not ready to accept any new frames.

Failure recovery. **A general OSI principle is that higher layers provide a means of recovery**

from the failure of lower layer functions. LAP-B provides recovery from failures at the physical layer (EIA232C or the communications medium) through its frame sequencing and acknowledgment scheme. If the communications line is disrupted, LAP-B effectively "remembers" the status of the link when it failed. When the communications line problem is corrected, the link can resume its transactions where it left off. Some PSDNs (especially private PSDNs) provide multiple physical paths between DTEs and DCEs so that if one physical path fails, an alternate path is automatically selected. Calls in progress over the failed link are not disconnected. Through mechanisms such as this one, PSDNs provide a high degree of availability.

(If you're hungry for more details on the above, refer to CCITT Recommendation X.25, Section 2.)

LAYER 3. THE NETWORK LAYER STANDARD: THE PACKET LAYER

The network layer peer protocol manages the transfer of data units called packets from one end of an X.25 connection to the other. Figure 8 shows the scope of the packet layer protocol compared to the scope of the layer 1 and layer 2 protocols.

OSI layer relationships in X.25 packet switching.

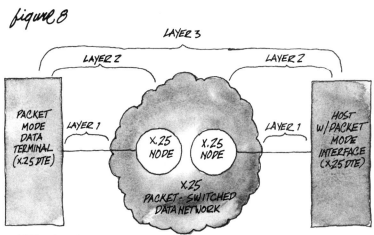

figure 8

LAYER 1 = CONNECTION TO CONNECTION   LAYER 2 = LINK TO LINK   LAYER 3 = END TO END

The physical and link layer protocols function on a connection-to-connection and link-to-link basis respectively, while the packet layer protocol functions on an end-to-end basis, connecting two DTEs across a PSDN. Its functions therefore reflect its *networking* role. The packet layer:

- establishes end-to-end connections
- addresses and routes, end-to-end
- performs end-to-end flow control
- releases network connections
- recovers from link layer (layer 2) failures
- provides optional network service features
- provides network diagnostic functions

Figure 9 shows the formation of an X.25 packet. The X.25 packet format and the LAP-B frame format have superficial similarities. In each case, a header area of overhead information is added to the end-user application data. The packet header contains networking information that is exchanged between two layer 3 peer entities.

Unlike the LAP-B peer protocol, with its two basic frame types, the X.25 packet layer protocol specifies many different packet types. Each packet type performs a certain layer 3 function. An indicator of the type of packet, and thus its function, is contained in the header information associated with each packet. Depending on the type of packet, the length of the header and its actual contents will vary considerably.

An X.25 packet consists of end user data and a header, containing information necessary to route the data accurately.

(More detailed information may be found in CCITT Recommendation X.25, Sections 3-7.)

Now for a closer look at some of the layer 3 functions.

figure 9

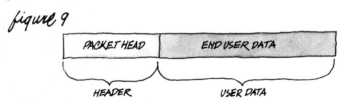

| PACKET HEAD | END USER DATA |

HEADER   USER DATA

Establishment of network connections. A group
of packet types called **call setup packets** establish
virtual circuits across a packet network. These packets'
headers contain the network addresses of the calling
and called DTEs, and thus specify the endpoints of a
requested X.25 connection. Routing tables in each
network node process this addressing information to
set up a virtual circuit between the endpoint addresses.
Once the virtual circuit has been established, the need
to specify its endpoint addresses in subsequent **data
packets** is eliminated.

End-to-end addressing and routing. Once a virtual circuit route has been assigned between two X.25
DTEs during call setup, each data packet holds information in its packet header about the call's route. This
information, called the logical channel number, takes
the place of the calling and called addresses for the duration of the virtual call. A logical channel number in a
packet header occupies much less space than full endpoint addresses, so it reduces overall network overhead.

End-to-end flow control. The mechanism of flow
control at the packet layer is similar to the mechanism
used at the link layer. Packets are assigned unique
sequence numbers, and there is a window size variable
limiting the number of packets that can be sent before
an acknowledgment is needed. By withholding acknowledgments when its buffers fill, the receiver can control
the rate at which the sender sends packets. Both link
layer and network layer flow control mechanisms operate independently and simultanenously. Packet layer
flow control is end-to-end rather than link-to-link (see
Figure 8).

Release of network connections. A group of X.25
packet types, called **call clearing packets** disconnect
a virtual circuit when the end users no longer require
a call. A field in the call clearing packet header is
used to indicate to both end users why the call has
been cleared.

Recovery from link layer (LAP-B) failures. In
accord with OSI's provision that higher layers provide
recovery from lower layer failures, the X.25 packet

The OSI provides that higher layer protocols provide recovery from lower layer failures. layer provides protection against link layer failures. The receiving DTE uses a packet's unique sequence number to acknowledge receipt of that packet or string of packets. In the case of a link layer failure along the path of a virtual circuit, the X.25 DTEs at either end of the circuit effectively "remember" the status of the virtual connection prior to the failure. So when an alternate link is provided to bypass the failed link, the virtual circuit can be returned to its condition immediately prior to the link failure. A group of X.25 packet types, called **reset packets**, recover end-to-end virtual circuits after link layer failures.

Optional network service features. X.25 defines a number of user facilities that affect the quality of service that PSN users can obtain. These user facilities fall into two categories:

- variable network attributes (e.g., packet size, window size)
- optional service features (e.g., closed user group, fast select)

(A complete list and detailed discussion of these optional user facilities is in CCITT Recommendation X.25, Section 6.)

When X.25 end users subscribe to a packet network, they can choose to be able to alter these attributes or invoke these features for each call. For example, an end user who wants increased packet throughput on a particular virtual call may request an increase in the layer 3 window size variable for that call. Requests for, and responses concerning, optional user facilities are contained in the headers of call setup packets.

Network diagnostics. The X.25 layer 3 protocol indicates to X.25 users the causes of various problems that they may encounter in trying to use the PSDN. For example, when an end user's procedural error clears a call, both end users are notified. Call clearing because of an improper user facility request is also reported,

28

as is call clearing due to such network problems as multiple link failures. CCITT Recommendation X.25, Annex E, contains a complete list of diagnostic indicators. These are located in the headers of call clearing packets, reset packets, and restart packets. In addition, a special type of packet, called a **diagnostic packet**, is used exclusively for this purpose.

ADDITIONAL CCITT X. RECOMMENDATIONS APPLICABLE TO PACKET SWITCHING

The CCITT has ratified a number of other X. recommendations pertaining to *public* packet switched data networks. Table 2 shows the X. number of each of these adjunct recommendations, their titles, and a brief statement of their scope and purpose.

A FEW WORDS ABOUT PROTOCOL CONVERSION

The process of packetizing and depacketizing data for transport over an X.25 network can be called protocol conversion only in the following sense: it converts a bit stream into X.25 format for shipment across the network. It does not convert one type of protocol into another: in other words, it can't make an async terminal look like an SDLC terminal. That kind of protocol conversion—more properly referred to as "protocol emulation"—requires the presence of additional DCE software before unlike devices can communicate across an X.25 (or any other) network.

The preceding discussion may contain more than you ever wanted to know about the X.25 protocol. Still, it makes abundantly clear why "packet switching" and "X.25" have come to be thought of as synonymous terms: for all practical purposes, it's the X.25 protocol that makes packet switching networks possible.

TABLE 2: ADDITIONAL CCITT RECOMMENDATIONS APPLICABLE TO PACKET SWITCHING

RECOMMENDATION #	TITLE	SCOPE/PURPOSE
X.3 Note 1	Packet Assembly/Disassembly Facility (PAD) in a Public Data Network	• a basic description of the packetizer/depacketizer functions through which *asynchronous* DTEs can access a packet network, • describes a number of PAD "parameters" (selectable functional modes), and shows the character codes that represent them, • provides for flexible support for a wide variety of asynchronous terminals on a public packet network.
X.21bis	Use on Public Data Networks of Data Terminal Equipment (DTE) Which is Designed for Interfacing to Synchronous V-series Modems	• describes the X.25 layer 1 peer protocol commonly used in North America
X.28 Note 1	DTE/DCE Interface for a Start-Stop Mode Data Terminal Equipment Accessing the Packet Assembly/Disassembly Facility (PAD) in a Public Data Network Situated in the Same Country	• describes the procedures (commands and responses) to be used between an asynchronous terminal and a X.3 PAD in a public packet network. • provides a detailed "user's manual" for users of asynchronous terminals on packet data networks (e.g., how to place a virtual call from the terminal, how to interpret mnemonic indicators received from the network).
X.29 Note 1	Procedures for the Exchange of Control Information and User Data Between a Packet Assembly/Disassembly (PAD) Facility and a Packet Mode DTE or Another PAD	• describes the procedures (commands and responses) to be used between an X.25 DTE (or a PAD) and an X.3 PAD in a public data network, • defines a group of packet types, and describes their command/response/transport functions, • provides a mechanism by which an X.25 DTE can control an X.3 PAD and, often, the asynchronous DTEs connected to it.
X.32 Note 2	Interface Between Data Terminal Equipment (DTE) and Data Circuit Terminating Equipment (DCE) for Terminals Operating in the Packet Mode and Accessing a Packet Switched Public Data Network Through a Public Switched Telephone Network or a Circuit Switched Data Network	• a dial-in/dial-out analog of X.25.
X.75	Terminal and Transit Call Control Procedures and Data Transfer System on International Circuits Between Packet Switched Data Networks	• describes physical, link and network layer protocols to be used on "gateway" connections *between* packet networks (usually thought of as being in different countries), • very similar to X.25 architecturally (i.e., OSI-compatible)
X.96	Call Progress Signals in Public Data Networks	• describes a multitude of call progress signals (status messages from the network) that may be encountered by the user of a public packet network.
X.121	International Numbering Plan for Public Data Networks	• describes a worldwide (or U.N. wide) addressing scheme for public data packet networks, • similar in concept to the scheme in place for the international voice telephone network,

NOTES:

General.— In addition to the Recommendations above, the die-hard reader is further referred to Recommendations X.1, X.2, X.4, X.15, X.21, X.24, X.31, X.135, X.136, each of which relates, albeit obliquely, to packet switching networks.

1—The three Recommendations X.3, X.28, and X.29 are often taken together as a group that describes the support of asynchronous terminals on a packet data network. For this reason, the asynchronous PAD facility described in these Recommendations is often call a "triple-X PAD"

4

PACKET
SWITCHING
APPLICATIONS

OR

when to take route X.25

If you live anywhere
other than Massachusetts, or maybe Rome,
you know that traffic flows best when people
observe the rules of the road rather than
treating them merely as suggestions. Conversely, to ensure data traffic flow, there are
certain suggestions you might want to treat
as rules, especially when it comes to deciding
whether or not to use packet switching. Although each
data communications application should be analyzed to
determine which communications technology best meets
its requirements, three general factors will determine
the benefit of packet switching in any application
(yes, even in Rome and Massachusetts):

- terminal population dispersion
- the need for connectivity
- traffic patterns and characteristics

31

Terminal population dispersion. The more
geographically dispersed the end user terminals are,
the more economical packet switching can be. Packet
networks take advantage of their ability to share
internodal trunk bandwidth among a number of users
simultaneously, thus reducing the cost per user. In a
circuit switched network, as the terminals move far-
ther away from the device to which they connect (a host
computer or another terminal), costs increase. In packet
switching networks, on the other hand, the terminals
are connected to PADs or other access devices, which
are physically close by. In other words, the cost to connect the end user over the local access connection is
limited to a short distance only.

The need for connectivity. The term **connectivity**
refers to the ability of a device to communicate with
other devices through a data communications facility.
The more devices an end user can reach from his or
her terminal, the greater the connectivity of that
terminal. Leased line networks, for example, usually
provide little connectivity because end users are hardwired to a host computer through a point-to-point or
multipoint line. By contrast, packet neworks usually
provide widespread connectivity. PSDNs provide virtual access from any network device to any other device
using the same protocol, assuming
that appropriate authorization-to-use
criteria have been met. The use of
standardized networking procedures,
such as X.25, also permits international connectivity over public PSDNs
by means of gateways.

**Packet switched
data networks pro-
vide virtual access
from any network
device to any other
device using the
same protocol.**

Traffic patterns and characteristics. The term
bursty has been used to describe the type of traffic
that PSDNs handle most economically and efficiently.
More meaningful terms, however, may be interactive or
transactional. Each of these terms suggests that PSDNs
fit best in low line usage applications. Such applications usually involve communications between a human
terminal operator and a host computer.

A human to host interaction is characterized by long gaps between successive data transmissions in both directions. A human operator generally needs a certain amount of idle time between data entries (e.g., while waiting to serve the next customer in a checkout line, to make decisions while standing in front of an ATM, to think about the next inquiry to a database). A host computer running an interactive application often serves more than one operator terminal simultaneously by timesharing. This introduces periods of idle time between successive transmissions to any one terminal. In these human-to-host interactions, PSDNs tend to be cost-effective because of their ability to multiplex data. Unlike dedicated bandwidth, which is assigned for some period of time regardless of whether or not it is actually used during that period, bandwidth on a packet switched network is used on a packet-by-packet basis.

TYPICAL "GOOD FIT" PACKET SWITCHING APPLICATIONS

To summarize, then, applications well-suited to PSDNs are those that are interactive or transactional, have geographically dispersed terminals, and benefit from a high degree of connectivity. Many such applications are in common use in every sector of modern society, and there is every indication that their number will increase in the future. A sampling of such "good fit" packet switching applications with which nearly everyone is familiar would include:

Inquiry/response applications:
- inquiries to corporate databases
- inquiries to public database providers
- inquiries to industry-specific databases
- electronic mail systems

Electronic funds transfer applications:
- automatic teller machines (ATMs)
- automated payroll deposit systems
- debit card transactions

Wholesale/retail applications:
- credit card approval systems
- point-of-sale transactions
- inventory control applications

Forms entry applications
- loan application processing
- insurance claims processing
- medical records processing

WHEN TO USE PUBLIC OR PRIVATE PSDNs

So far this discussion of appropriate packet switching applications has omitted consideration of public versus private packet switching networks. That's because we've been focusing on the *kinds* of applications that are best suited to packet switching. Whether the PSDN used is public or private depends not so much on the kind of application as on the *volume* of data traffic the application needs to support. Thus applications in the banking and financial industries, for example, often must support volumes of traffic large enough to cost-justify installation of a private X.25 network. Which network is right for your applications should be determined in conjunction with an X.25 specialist experienced in network design. (A more extended discussion of reasons for building a private X.25 network will be found in Chapter 6.)

Whether the PSDN used is public or private depends not so much on the *kind* of application as on the *volume* of traffic it needs to support.

What follows are four typical scenarios, involving both public and private packet switching networks. They're intended to demonstrate the range and variety of X.25 solutions available today and to help you start thinking about how packet switching might be profitable for your own data communications network.

REDUCING PUBLIC DATA NETWORK (PDN) ACCESS CHARGES

In this example, a real estate firm with a number of local offices is using Codex asynchronous X.25 PADs to reduce the number of phone lines needed to access the PDN. Each PAD can connect multiple async ports to the PDN using just one phone line. Additional line cost savings can be realized when locations are geographically remote from each other, such as locations D and E. Should the volume of traffic increase to a level that would cost-justify installation of a private data network, Codex packet switches would provide a cost-effective alternative to the PDN.

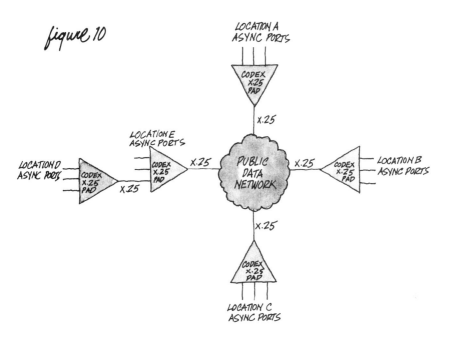

figure 10

REDUCING DATA TRANSPORT COSTS

Here the cost of using the PDN had become excessive for a university with a large number of terminals distributed among various departments and campuses. To solve this problem, the university installed a private X.25 network using a combination of Codex packet switches and PADs. Codex multiplexers and leased line modems also feed data traffic into the network, which is managed by a Codex network management system.

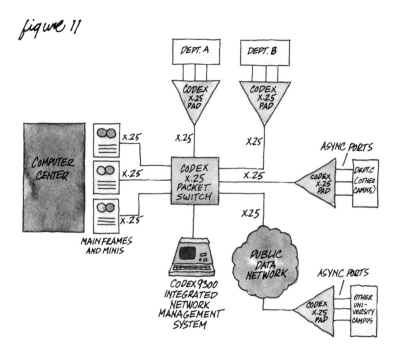

figure 11

PROVIDING REDUNDANCY AND AVAILABILITY

In this example, a major financial institution has created an X.25 backbone network using Codex X.25 backbone nodes at key data center locations around the world. In addition to their capacity to carry heavy volumes of data traffic, Codex backbone nodes also provide dynamic routing, which prevents a single point of failure from disrupting the flow of information. The nodes ensure that when necessary, traffic will be rerouted transparently to the user.

figure 12

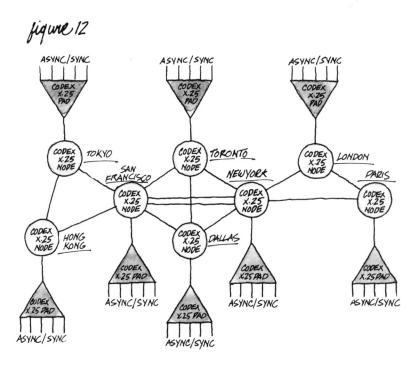

INTEGRATING X.25 INTO A DIGITAL NETWORK

Here a Fortune 100 company with a Codex T1/E1 backbone is using X.25 as a cost-effective way of concentrating data traffic within the network. By taking advantage of packet switching's connectivity and low-cost remote access, as well as efficient gateways into the backbone network, the user now has the best of both technologies. Codex packet switches with frame relay interfaces act as feeders into the digital backbone, while Codex flexible networking exchanges are used to channel IBM traffic into the X.25 network.

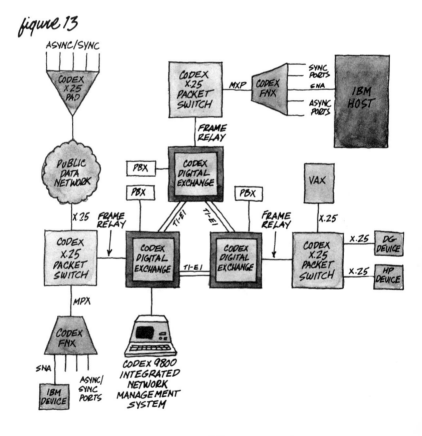

figure 13

5

PACKET SWITCHING BENEFITS

OR

you be the judge

OK, you've listened patiently to the evidence in favor of X.25 networking. Now it's time to sit in judgment. In this chapter we'll focus largely on the *network benefits* of using X.25 packet switching. First, however, let's review the overall *business benefits,* such as those enjoyed by the X.25 users whose applications were discussed in the last chapter. These business benefits fall into four main categories:

Increased revenue. In businesses such as the financial services industry, where the network is a critical part of the business transaction itself, X.25 can actually help increase revenues. That's because increased nonproprietary connectivity allows you to combine multiple networks and bring new users online without sacrificing quality of service. In other words, an X.25 network enables you more easily to expand your customer base, thereby generating additional revenues.

Increased level of service. By ensuring greater reliability, resiliency, and redundancy, an X.25 network helps you provide both your customers and network operators with a more consistent level of service.

Decreased operating costs. As we've seen, X.25 packet switching can reduce the day to day costs of operating your network for a number of reasons: facilities are shared by multiple users, sync and async are supported on the same X.25 device, an X.25 network allows for multiple host vendor support.

Cost-effective network growth. X.25 networking facilitates economical expansion of your network by eliminating dependence on proprietary protocols and allowing you to choose products from vendors who can offer you the best solutions.

These business benefits grow directly out of the network benefits made possible by X.25 packet switching. How do you measure those networking advantages? By using the same criteria you'd use to judge the benefits of any data communications technology:

- connectivity
- availability
- accuracy
- flexibility
- security
- manageability
- expandability
- cost-effectiveness

What follows is a brief review of each of these criteria—just to make sure we're all judging by the same standards. If you already feel comfortable with the terms, please feel free to proceed to the next section of this chapter, on migration to packet switching.

Connectivity. As noted in the last chapter, connectivity is the ability of a device to communicate with other devices through a data communications facility. Although a high degree of connectivity is not required in certain applications (e.g., host-to-host file transfers), **increases in connectivity are usually accompanied by decreases in equipment cost.** For example, if a terminal that is used to access applications on one host computer can also be used to access other hosts, the need for multiple terminals is eliminated, lowering the overall cost to the end user.

Availability. Availability is the probability that a communications facility will provide the connectivity required by an end user **when it is needed.** Sometimes referred to (incorrectly) as "reliability" or (correctly) as "uptime", availability is expressed as the percentage of time that the facility will provide the desired connectivity to an end user. For example, a data communications facility that is rated as being "99.95% available" will be able to provide connectivity to an end user for all but 263 minutes over a one-year period (less than one unavailable minute per day).

Accuracy. Accuracy is the ability of a datacomm facility to reproduce exactly at its output that which was presented to its input. Easily measured in instances where protocol conversion does not occur, accuracy is typically expressed in terms of some number of error occurrences per unit volume of data transported. Often encountered units of measurement include bit-error rate (BER), character-error rate (CER), block error rate (BLER), and packet error rate (PER). For example, a datacomm facility advertised as having a BER of 1×10^{-6} is advertising that only one in a million bits transported will be corrupted between the sender and the receiver. As with availability, increases in accuracy are always viewed as beneficial. Furthermore, in applications such as electronic funds transfers, accuracy of transport may be an overriding factor in the choice of a particular data transport technology.

Flexibility. Flexibility is the capacity of data-comm facility to be adapted to meet the specific requirements of a particular end user application. Flexibility can take on many forms. For instance, an end user may wish to alter the grade of service from time to time in an effort to reduce transport costs for noncritical transmissions. In general, flexibility can be thought of as value that is added to the transport task by the data communications facility.

Security. Security refers to the ability of a datacomm facility to protect itself from unwanted intrusion by unauthorized users, either within or outside the network. Usually some security is provided at the application or session level, typically through a Closed User Group feature. In some applications, such as those involving government classified data, security may be the primary factor in choosing one particular data transport technology over another.

Manageability. Manageability is the degree to which the owner/operator of datacomm facility has administrative and maintenance control over that facility. Can problems be diagnosed easily? Once diagnosed, can corrective measures be taken without dispatching a technician to a remote location? Are measures of facility performance being compiled and updated continuously in order to uncover potential problem areas or to serve as a guideline for expansion planning? Are detailed usage records for each end user available to facilitate billing and/or accounting functions? **Increased manageability can decrease day-to-day operating costs and enhance the network's quality of service.**

Expandability. Expandability is the ease with which the owner/operator of a datacomm facility can increase the capacity of the facility to meet increased data transport demand and to accommodate additional end user devices. Because the owner/operator often owns the host application as well, expandability can refer to the cost of expanding the connectivity of that application, thereby permitting access from a larger number of end user terminals. **Ease of expansion at**

low cost is beneficial to the owners, operators, and end users of a datacomm facility.

Cost-effectiveness. Unless another factor, such as security or accuracy is of overriding importance, **the bottom line cost usually determines the data transport technology for a given application.** This cost is the sum of many component parts, including:

- hardware and software costs (e.g., terminals, modems, PADs, switching nodes, network management components, etc.)
- communications facility costs (e.g., leased lines, dial-up message units, packet usage charges)
- administration and maintenance costs

Fortunately, making a choice based on cost is usually easy. A straightforward cost comparison, although sometimes complex, yields accurate figures upon which a decision can be made.

Those are the comparative criteria. The remainder of this chapter will show that the use of packet switching can result in substantial cost reductions in many applications. In these cases, the other benefits of packet technology (such as increased accuracy and flexibility) are merely added incentives to make the transition to X.25 networking.

**MIGRATION TO PACKET SWITCHING:
A COMPARATIVE BENEFITS ANALYSIS**
What follows is a detailed analysis of the benefits of migrating to X.25 in an inquiry/response application. We'll begin by looking at the application itself, then compare the "before" and "after" using the measurement criteria defined above.

The application. A large financial services company sells a wide variety of services off its network. Figure 14 shows one geographic region of the company. Before the migration to X.25, the network consisted of multi-drop SDLC and dial-in async users who connected with their respective hosts (only one of the hosts is shown here) via a public offering (an 800 service in the U.S.). This meant the company was paying for a lot of bandwidth they weren't always using, had poor response time for corporate users, and dedicated calls for dial-up users.

Now, using X.25, subscribers to the company's services dial in to remote X.25 PADs from either an async terminal or PADs running 3270 emulation software. In addition, corporate users log on via 3270 type terminals or local area networks.

This backbone network provides a single resource for transportation. To the async dial-in user, it provides an X.25 PAD function and allows the terminal to log on to the host of choice. (Note that once it arrives at the host it may need to undergo protocol emulation as discussed above, page 29. This could involve software on the host or communications controller, or it could be done by an additional hardware/software component.)

A simplified view of an X.25 migration in an inquiry/response application.

figure 14

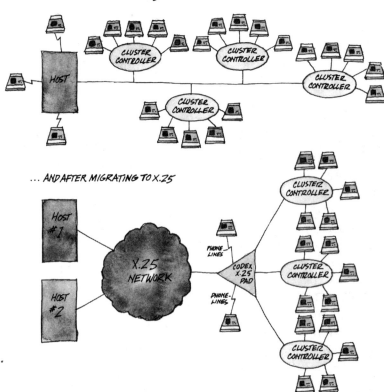

BEFORE MIGRATING TO X.25 ...

... AND AFTER MIGRATING TO X.25

The 3270 bit streams from both the PCs and 3270 terminals are packetized in an X.25 format and then shipped across the network to the destination. Upon arrival, these bit streams enter the host environment either in native SDLC format or in X.25 via a software package that reformats the X.25 packet into the QLLC layer of SDLC.

Overall, then, the migration saved the company both money and bandwidth. A look at our geographic region will show in greater detail why the migration to X.25 was desirable.

Connectivity before X.25. Before the deployment of X.25, each SDLC user terminal was connected via its cluster controller to only one host. Dial-in users wanting to access one host and then another were obliged to go through a hang-up and redial process that could take as long as 15 seconds to complete. Plus as the number of dial-in users increased, the host FEP (not shown) had to provide additional ports to meet the demand.

Connectivity with X.25. A terminal operator, using the proper packet addresses, can now access any host on the network, if authorized. Once a connection is established with a PAD, dial-in async terminal users can access multiple hosts sequentially without hang-up and redial procedures. (This time-saving feature is especially helpful in applications such as credit card approvals.)

Availability before X.25. For SDLC users, availability was all or nothing. When a channel failed, availability dropped to 0% for the time necessary to repair it. For dial-in users, availability depended on the carrier. Generally speaking, as a channel's length increased, the probability of mechanical failure (physical breakage) and electrical failure (noise from external equipment) increased too.

Availability with X.25. As we indicated in Chapter 2, PSDNs are designed for maximum availability. When packet switching nodes are deployed in a redundant or "standby" configuration, the failure of a single node in a redundant pair does not cause interruption of service. Nodes are also usually set up in a mesh configuration with redundant links (see Figure 3), providing extensive alternate routing capabilities. Finally, as we've also seen, most PSDNs use a layered protocol set (X.25) in which higher layers offer protection from lower layer failures. For devices connected to a PSDN through X.25 channels, load sharing over redundant channels further increases overall network resilience.

Accuracy before X.25. Data accuracy depended on both line quality and the modem technology employed. (To simplify Figure 14, the modems have been omitted.)

Accuracy with X.25. The link (LAP-B) layer of the X.25 protocol performs error control. You'll remember that data frames are copied from one node to the next as they progress through the packet network. Using this layer 2 procedure, X.25 packet networks achieve packet error rates (PER) of better than one errored packet in one billion packets transported (i.e., 1×10^{-9} PER). Note, however, that local access connections from the end user terminals to the packet network are usually telco-provided analog channels, and these are not protected by link layer error control procedures. For this reason the choice of PAD or other access device is crucial. (We just happen to know of an excellent X.25 supplier, but more on that later.)

Flexibility before X.25. Once the network was deployed, there was virtually no flexibility in how it was used.

Flexibility with X.25. Now the company has a wide range of optional services to choose from. Present generation packet switching technology is extensively software driven, permitting the network to be adapted to specific datacomm requirements. For example, CCITT Recommendation X.25 defines a standard list of optional user facilities (Table 3) by which users can affect network performance. Beyond these standard options, many providers support proprietary optional features, such as call setup priority, which can enhance the flexibility of a given application.

Security before X.25. Although add-on security measures, such as encryption devices and dial-back modems may be judged indispensable in sensitive data applications, we'll focus here on the security of the transport system itself. In our example, the host computer had to provide its own security scheme whose integrity depended on the integrity of individual users.

TABLE 3: OPTIONAL USER FACILITIES (FEATURES) AVAILABLE ON X.25 PACKET SWITCHING NETWORKS

FACILITY NAME	SEE CCITT X.25 SECTION
On-Line Facility Registration	6.1
Extended Packet Sequence Numbering	6.2
D Bit Modification	6.3
Packet Retransmission	6.4
Incoming Calls Barred	6.5
Outgoing Calls Barred	6.6
One-Way Logical Channel Outgoing	6.7
One-Way Logical Channel Incoming	6.8
Non-Standard Default Packet Sizes	6.9
Non-Standard Default Window Sizes	6.10
Default Throughput Classes Assignment	6.11
Flow Control Parameter Negotiation	6.12
Throughput Class Negotiation	6.13
Closed User Groups	6.14
Bilateral Closed User Groups	6.15
Fast Select	6.16
Fast Select Acceptance	6.17
Reverse Charging	6.18
Reverse Charging Acceptance	6.19
Local Charging Prevention	6.20
Network User Identification	6.21
Charging Information	6.22
RPOA Selection	6.23
Hunt Group	6.24
Call Redirection	6.25
Called Line Address Modified Notification	6.26
Call Redirection Notification	6.27
Transit Delay Selection and Indication	6.28

Security with X.25. Loss of security is countered with two optional user facilities, Network User Identification (NUI) and Closed User Groups (CUG). For further information on these facilities, see the corresponding CCITT X.25 Recommendation sections listed in Table 3.

Manageability before X.25. This depended primarily on the modems used. If low-cost, "plain vanilla" modems were used, the network had a decentralized diagnostic capability, such as loopback testing. Network control modems (such as those used by the company in our example and those we at Codex recommend for many critical leased line applications) offer greater functionality, including monitoring, testing, and configuring both local and remote devices within the modem network.

Manageability with X.25. You'll recall that in Chapter 1, the network management center was introduced as the central point of control for all of the network's switching and access nodes. Nearly all PSDN equipment suppliers offer centralized or semi-centralized network management systems which perform functions such as those listed on page 7. Clearly, compared to the management functions available on a typical dial network, the management tools available on a PSDN provide strong justification to migrate to packet switching—and were in fact a primary consideration for our financial services company.

Expandability before X.25. To begin with, the multi-drop lines had become overpopulated, resulting in slow response times. Moreover, while a number of dial-in users can contend for a single host FEP port (not shown), additional dial-in ports on the FEPs may be required if a large number of new dial-in terminals is added.

Expandability with X.25. X.25 supports multiple simultaneous virtual calls over a single physical channel. Each new X.25 link supports a certain number of new terminals (a 1:X ratio), depending on the traffic characteristics of the particular host application. Thus the corporate users had increased response time and better management of growth in the network. The use of X.25 also makes expansion more predictable on the host side of the network because statistical data provided by the network management center can be used to determine when host access capacity will be exceeded— again of special importance in our sample application.

Cost-effectiveness before X.25. For the region in our example, costs included:

- terminals
- speed-compatible dial-up modems
- cluster controllers
- usage cost of the private offering (800 service·in the U.S.)
- maintenance of the multi-drop network

As already noted, the indirect cost of wasted bandwidth on the private offering must also be taken into account.

Cost-effectiveness with X.25. Costs for the region now include:

- terminals
- speed-compatible dial-up modems
- cluster controllers
- a PAD local to the region
- shared usage cost of the private network

For our financial services company, then, migration to packet switching results in two areas of cost savings. First, the cost of maintaining the multidrop network has been eliminated. This savings far outweighs the combined cost of the PAD and dial-up access to the packet network. Second, as more users are added to the network, the PSDN becomes much cheaper than the private offering—plus there's no wasted bandwidth and better management of network growth.

Note: Because of the variable usage charges associated with a packet network, an accurate assessment of the absolute amount of savings in any realword application can only be derived from a detailed comparative cost analysis.

PACKET SWITCHING BENEFITS: A SUMMARY
The table below summarizes the *potential* benefits of migration to a packet switching network. Naturally, each application presents a unique set of circumstances, requirements, and budgetary constraints. Often, however, close analysis will demonstrate that packet switching provides the best and most cost-effective solution.

TABLE 4. MIGRATION TO PACKET SWITCHING: A SUMMARY

FACILITY ATTRIBUTE	FOR DIRECT CONNECTS	FOR DIAL-UPS
Connectivity	Increased	Increased
Availability	Increased	Little effect
Accuracy	Increased	Increased
Flexibility	Increased	Increased
Security	Little effect	Increased
Manageability	Increased	Increased
Expandability	Increased	Increased
Cost-effectiveness	Increased	Increased

6

PACKET SWITCHING IN A PRIVATE WIDE AREA NETWORK OR

don't let your WAN make you wan

You'll recall that in the Introduction we mentioned that there are three types of packet switching networks: public, private, and hybrid. In Chapter 4, you saw examples of these networks in the four applications shown (Figures 10 through 13). For most smaller or "entry-level" applications, you'll find the public data network to be well-suited to your requirements. But what if you have a much larger network with many more demands being made on your resources? The answer is that packet switching can improve network performance and reduce costs.

This chapter focuses more specifically on some of the benefits of packet switching in a private wide area networking environment.

51

WHY BUILD A PRIVATE X.25 NETWORK?

There are some very good reasons for building a private X.25 data network. Most of these reasons have been covered earlier, but it might be useful to summarize them here in the context of this discussion of private wide area networking.

Cost reduction. A private X.25 network reduces transmission costs by allowing multiple applications to share the same phone lines. It also lowers central site hardware costs because the X.25 protocol provides for a single-line interface to front-end processors and host computers.

Standards support. Using an internationally recognized standard network interface protects your network investment over time. It simplifies network growth, allowing you to integrate computer systems and architectures from different X.25-compatible vendors into a single network.

Bandwidth optimization and efficiency. When you use a dedicated circuit for low line usage applications, bandwidth is wasted during the pauses between transactions. With X.25 you only use the bandwidth you really need—when you need it. Further efficiency is ensured through sharing of network transmission facilities and resources by multiple host types and applications.

In a private X.25 network you use only the bandwidth you really need— when you need it.

Improved connectivity. X.25 increases your ability to support both intercorporate and interdepartmental networking. Instead of being able to access only those applications resident on an attached host, users can now access any protocol-compatible host on the network as well as compatible host applications outside the private network.

Integration into public networks. X.25 also provides internetworking with public data networks via gateways plus easy migration to future offerings such as ISDN.

Figures 11 and 13 in Chapter 4 show some of these benefits in action. They also show you how a private X.25 network can be effectively integrated with multiple networking technologies (such as T1/E1) as well as with products from different networking vendors. In this chapter, we want to take a more detailed look at how packet switching can benefit a private wide area networking application, in this case a polled multipoint networking environment.

PACKET SWITCHING IN MULTIPOINT ENVIRONMENTS

Figure 15 shows a traditional polled multipoint environment. A host computer/front end processor (FEP) complex supports a population of end user terminals, attached through cluster controllers. The terminals connect to the FEP via telco-provided multipoint analog leased lines.

In a traditional polled multipoint environment, a host computer/FEP complex supports a population of end user terminals, attached through cluster controllers.

figure 15

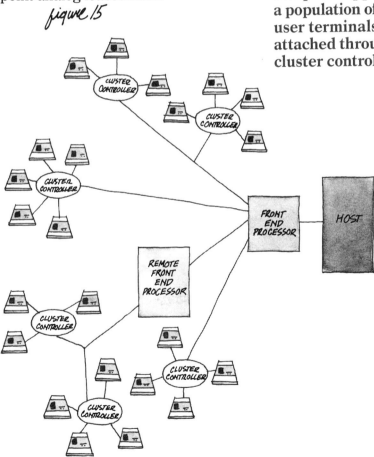

53

The FEP controls talker/listener relationships on each multipoint line through a **polling** technique. The FEP sequentially polls the terminals connected to it, asking whether or not they have data to be sent to the host. The FEP waits for a response from that terminal before polling the next terminal. This polling technique, developed in the 1960s, was an early attempt to conserve costly bandwidth by having many terminals share a single multipoint line.

A number of real-world data communications applications (roughly 80%) still reside on multipoint polling networks and many of these (e.g., medical records, applications processing, ATMs) have characteristics that make them ideally suited to a packet switching environment. In addition, because many manufacturers are discontinuing support for their polled protocol offerings, these applications are prime candidates for migration to a PSDN.

POLLING ENVIRONMENTS: THREE MAJOR DRAWBACKS

Although multipoint polling schemes do provide facility conservation, they suffer from three major drawbacks when compared to later generation networking technologies such as packet switching:

- lack of connectivity
- resource intensiveness
- cost

Lack of connectivity. Figure 15 shows that each operator terminal is essentially hardwired to the host FEP and is thus able to access only applications resident on that host. In order to access applications on other protocol-compatible hosts, an operator must have multiple terminals, each of which is connected to the appropriate host through an entirely separate network. This lack of connectivity often leads to the cumbersome and costly proliferation of many separate but parallel networks.

In contrast to packet switching, multipoint polling schemes lack connectivity. Moreover, they are resource intensive and costly to deploy, maintain, and expand.

54

Resource intensiveness. In polling environments, every terminal must be in constant contact with its FEP to listen for and respond to its polls. Therefore all terminals are active simultaneously and there is no real "busy hour" in a multipoint polled network. Moreover, the FEP must allocate a portion of its internal resources to the creation of a software image of each real terminal. These images are often called virtual terminals. As the number of real terminals in the network increases, the number of virtual terminals that must be defined to the FEP also increases until the capacity of the FEP is reached. This is true regardless of how many terminals actually require simultaneous connection to the host for the purpose of exchanging end user data.

Furthermore, any time that a terminal is added to the network, removed from the network, or moved within the network, the FEP must be modified to reflect the change. This modification process, known as FEP regeneration, is often time and labor intensive.

Finally, depending on the number of terminals supported by a multipoint line, up to 30% of the capacity of that line may be used to support the polling process itself (up to 1440 bps on a 4800 bps line). Thus considering both FEP and line capacity, polling technologies are resource intensive.

Cost. The polling protocol in a multipoint environment makes these networks costly to deploy, maintain, and expand. Like point-to-point leased lines, multipoint lines are leased on a distance sensitive basis. They are typically more costly than point-to-point lines of the same length, depending on the number of drops (the number of terminals supported) on the line. By migrating polled multipoint applications to a PSDN, these drawbacks can be reduced substantially.

SUPPORT OF MULTIPOINT POLLING PROTOCOLS ON A PSDN

Figure 16 shows the Figure 15 host and terminals after migration to a PSDN. The host/FEP complex attaches to a PAD within the PSDN by telco-provided leased analog lines (point-to-point). The number of channels depends on the traffic volume to be supported by the FEP during peak times (busy hour).

The leased lines supporting the terminal population (including cluster controllers) have been reconfigured substantially upon migration to the packet network. The purpose of this reconfiguration is to take full advantage of the widespread deployment of PSDN PADs (not shown). In some cases, the multipoint lines have been eliminated entirely, based on distance and cost. These have been replaced by multiple point-to-point lines. In other cases, multipoint lines have been maintained, though with fewer drops than before. In either case, the leased lines supporting the controllers and terminals connect PADs within the packet network. Note that the remote FEP that performed a concentration function in Figure 15 has been eliminated by the packet network. Now the PSDN concentrates traffic from outlying groups of terminals to the host FEP.

To permit communication between the host/FEP complex and

In a packet switched data network, the host/FEP attaches to a PAD within the PSDN, eliminating the need for a direct connection between each terminal and its FEP.

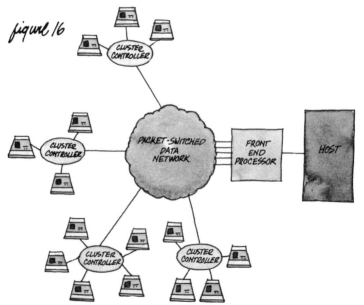

figure 16

56

the terminal population in Figure 16, the PSDN performs three activities: polling emulation, protocol transport, and address mapping.

Polling emulation. Polling data, which is actually continuous overhead, may account for up to 30% of the total traffic transported on a multipoint network. Clearly, having overhead information, rather than end user data, occupying 30% of your bandwidth is not the ideal way to use the network. Therefore polling data should be prevented from crossing the PSDN. The packet network accomplishes this through a technique called emulation, shown in Figure 17.

Briefly, it works this way. Within the PSDN, the PAD functions are asymmetric in the multipoint polling environment. A host PAD connects the host/FEP complex to the network, and a terminal PAD connects the cluster controllers and terminals to the network.

The host PAD emulates the polling functions of the cluster controller/terminal by responding to polls from the host FEP. The terminal PAD emulates the polling functions of the host FEP by polling the cluster controllers/terminals. Thus the host FEP *thinks* that it is still polling a population of real clusters/terminals, and the clusters/terminals *think* that they are still communicating with the FEP. Instead they are exchanging polls and responses with the appropriate emulation software in the PADs. This emulation technique handles polling locally and is sometimes known as **spoofing**. Polling data does not traverse the PSDN.

Protocol transport. A packet network transport protocol, as shown in Figure 17, carries data in one protocol (the native protocol) across the network by means of a second protocol (usually X.25). In this process, the native protocol's original functionality should remain intact. When the transport protocol functions properly, end users are not aware of the PSDN's presence between their terminals and the host FEP.

When an end user terminal has data to send to the host in response to a poll from the terminal PAD, the transport protocol establishes a virtual circuit to the appropriate host PAD across the packet network and transfers the user data into a buffer in the host PAD packet by packet. In response to a poll from the FEP, the user data is transferred from the host PAD to the host. This completes the data transfer from terminal to host. The transport protocol is the glue that binds the terminal PAD and the host PAD together and permits local polling.

Address mapping. Address mapping is used to establish a virtual circuit between two devices (usually a terminal and host application) by creating a temporary logical association between polling addresses and packet network addresses. Address mapping is initiated by the terminal PAD during call setup. When a session with a host application is requested by the end user, the terminal PAD prompts the user to enter that application's packet destination address. The terminal PAD then associates the cluster and device addresses (polling address) of the originating terminal with a virtual circuit number assigned for the virtual connection. Data flowing to and from that terminal is thus routed on the appropriate virtual circuit.

A packet network transport protocol carries data in one protocol (the native protocol) across the network by means of a second protocol (X.25).

figure 17

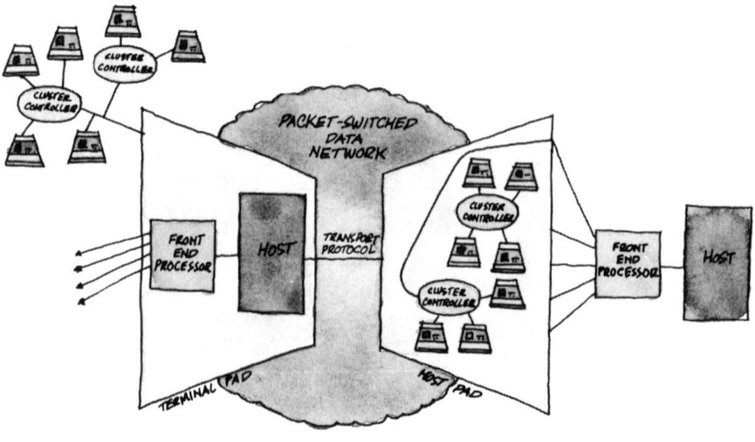

At the host end, a similar process occurs between the host PAD and the application during call acceptance. Routing within the packet network proceeds as usual. Once a virtual connection route has been established between two specific device addresses, it remains for the duration of the call.

THE BENEFITS OF PACKET SWITCHING IN A POLLED MULTIPOINT ENVIRONMENT

The above example demonstrates some of the advantages of packet switching in private wide area networking applications that we summarized earlier, especially:

Connectivity enhancement. By performing polling emulation and address mapping, the packet switched data network permits an end user to access multiple protocol-compatible host computers from a single operator terminal.

Conservation of host/FEP resources. Polling emulation, as performed by the host PAD in the PSDN, eliminates the need for continuous contact between each operator terminal and its FEP to exchange polling information. The FEP exchanges polling information with the host PAD only. Looking at some numbers drives the point home. Let's say a host FEP supports a population of 100 terminals in a traditional leased line multipoint environment. No more than 25 of these, however, are in session at any one time with host applications software. In a traditional configuration, all 100 terminals need to be defined to the FEP to support polling functions. In the packet environment, however, only 25 virtual terminals need to be defined in the host PAD and consequently in the FEP. Therefore the PSDN reduces resource requirements in the FEP by 75%. The PSDN permits four times as many terminals to use the same FEP resources. In addition, changes to the terminal population (adds, deletes, moves) no longer require a complete regeneration of the FEP software. They are now accommodated easily by a PSDN map update.

In a PSDN, changes to the terminal population no longer require a complete regeneration of the FEP software.

Cost reduction. As we've just seen, migration of a polled multipoint application from a leased line circuit environment to a PSDN conserves costly FEP hardware and software resources and reduces FEP maintenance costs. In addition, line reconfiguration provides significant cost savings on the terminal side of the network because long multipoint lines are shortened, and the average number of drops per line decreases. Often, in fact, multipoint lines are reduced to point-to-point connections.

STATISTICAL MULTIPLEXING VS. PACKET SWITCHING: HOW TO CHOOSE

Another question asked by private wide area networking managers is whether to choose statistical time division multiplexing (STDM) or X.25 packet switching for a particular application. After all, both are packet-based concentration and switching technologies. So how do you decide?

Let's start with a short comparison. Statistical multiplexing (or "stat muxing") is a concentration and switching scheme that allocates bandwidth only as terminals require it. Stat muxing uses addressing schemes which lend themselves to efficient bandwidth utilization and low throughput delay. These features make stat muxing highly effective in hierarchical, point-to-point topologies with little need for external connectivity.

The X.25 interface, on the other hand, is an international **standard** protocol which evolved out of the need to connect geographically dispersed computing sites with multiple computer vendors and to optimize the sharing of resources within the network. Within X.25 networks, remote users usually have the capability to communicate with one another within a distributed data processing architecture. X.25 networks are often hybrid public/private networks which can be expanded easily to accommodate new users.

Both statistical multiplexing and X.25 packet switching provide networking advantages when used in the appropriate applications.

Both stat muxing and X.25 packet switching provide networking advantages when they are used with the appropriate applications. Here are how two imaginary users might implement these technologies to provide important business benefits for their companies.

WHY A CABLE TV FIRM CHOSE STATISTICAL MULTIPLEXING

A major cable company manages more than 60 cable systems nationwide. The company maintains a national network including stat mux nodes transmitting data to 800 terminals at 70 offices throughout the country.

The network configuration is point-to-point from a central processing facility to nine regional hub sites. At the hub sites, stat mux nodes concentrate data over tail circuits to regional offices throughout the country. These nodes replace an older configuration in which the company ran point-to-point lines from the central data center to approximately 70 nationwide offices.

Ninety percent of network traffic is async, terminating in a host supporting customer service functions such as billing, collections, service dispatch, and pay per view home movies. The remaining 10 percent of traffic is synchronous, supporting corporate financial operations such as general ledger inquiry and reporting.

When upgrading the network, the company considered both statistical multiplexing and X.25 packet switching. The following factors entered into their decision to go with the former:

Cost savings. The stat mux solution allowed the company to change its network configuration, implement the nine regional hub sites, and replace the former point-to-point lines with shorter, more economical tail circuits running off the nodes. The new configuration reduced leased line costs from $62,000 to $41,000 per month. This savings alone financed the cost of the new multiplexing equipment.

Ability to prioritize async and sync traffic within the network. After testing several stat mux and X.25 switches, the company's Datacomm Manager chose a stat mux switching node offering a reliable prioritization scheme for preventing sync traffic from overrunning async during transmission. Since most of their traffic is async, this prioritization scheme was an important consideration.

Efficiency. Stat muxing offered 80% line utilization without serious degrading, compared to 70% to 75% for X.25 packet switching, in tests run before the purchase decision was made.

Ease of installation and maintenance. Office personnel plug in and turn on the company's stat mux switching node; technicians do the remaining work from the data center.

WHY A MAJOR MANUFACTURER CHOSE X.25 PACKET SWITCHING

A major North American manufacturer is upgrading its switching technology from stat muxing to an X.25 packet switched network. This change is part of the company's plans to build a new nationwide network that will offer connectivity to offices worldwide while providing increased capabilities for the company's U.S. customer service organization.

The company's hosts are located at a data center in Blue Eye, Arkansas, with remote switching sites in Mist, Oregon, and Mattawamkeag, Maine. The network currently supports 300 users; the company wants to double this number during the coming year.

This network supports customer service operations by tracking service parts inventory and transmitting data for online service dispatch. The network also supports internal administrative operations, including contract billing and accounts payable and receivable.

Within the next few years, the company plans to offer its customers the option of accessing the company's network to track its progress on service calls. In addition, a separate X.25 network provides data transmission for the Electronic Funds Transfer Division, which provides online credit verification for retail outlets. The company expects to realize the following benefits from its X.25 network:

The ability to connect new users to its worldwide network with ease was a principal factor in a major manufacturer's decision to implement an X.25 network.

Ease in connecting new users to the network.
Since the company plans to offer customers the option
of accessing its network, this feature is especially
important. Instead of reprogramming multiplexers, it's
easier to give customers a new telephone number and
have them connect to the network over the public X.25
network.
*Connectivity with the company's worldwide infor-
mation network.*
Compliance with a standard protocol. This provides more flexibility in vendor selection, since packet
switching equipment from different vendors will talk to
one another as part of the X.25 protocol.
High degree of rerouting flexibility in case of a
disaster or some other occurrence requiring rerouting.
Less hardware. The company now has a single
line interface to connect directly to the host ports
via X.25.
Compatibility with leading edge applications
including Electronic Data Interchange (EDI).

STATISTICAL MULTIPLEXING VS. PACKET SWITCHING: A SUMMARY

So there you have it. Each of these two networking
technologies is based on the packetization of data. The
important distinction between them lies in the networking problems they are designed to address.

Note: Codex's stat muxing capabilities include products that combine statistical multiplexing and X.25 processing.

The Codex 6742 and 6745 Flexible Networking Exchanges combine statistical multiplexing and X.25 processing capabilities.

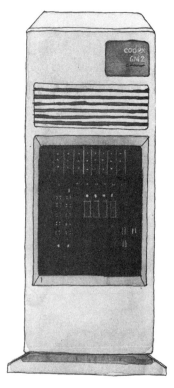
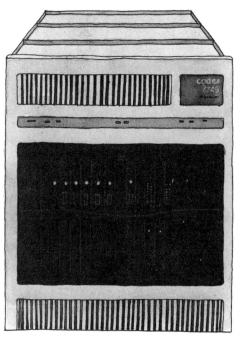

THE FUTURE OF PACKET SWITCHING

a few notes

With the proliferation of personal computers, which are often used as intelligent data terminals, communications applications for PCs are rapidly multiplying. The success of these applications will depend on the availability of cost-effective data transport. Many such applications fit well in a PSDN environment because they involve a geographically dispersed terminal population and the need to exchange short messages. What follows are a few examples.

ELECTRONIC MAIL
Electronic mail systems, when first introduced in the 1970s, usually involved localized populations of users, often within a building or across a campus. Local area networks (LANs) best served these systems. However, in cases in which wide-area E-mail systems are in use (national corporations with multiple office locations across a coun-

try), packet switching has become popular as a cost-effective means to connect multiple local electronic mail systems, often through interconnection of the LANs on which they reside.

Many public value-added network (VAN) providers have recently introduced electronic mail offerings for use by the general public. As the cost of transferring hard-copy messages by traditional means continues to increase, and as electronic mail systems are made available to more and more end user terminals through PSDNs, the use of packet technology will continue to grow. With its availability, accuracy, connectivity and cost advantages, packet switching is likely to be indispensable to E-mail applications for years to come.

VIDEOTEX

Videotex providers offer such varied services as remote electronic banking, airline reservations, electronic shopping, stock market transactions, electronic mail, games and education. All videotex services, however, share certain characteristics, including:

- interactive communication with a database of stored information
- end user control of the information provided (inquiry/ response)
- provision of information to mass markets at low end user cost
- provision of a user friendly interface to the database (usually menu oriented)

With the exception of a few isolated application databases offered by information service providers such as CompuServe, videotex has not been offered seriously in the United States. Most European countries, however, have had government-run videotex services in place for some time now. Two of the most successful of these are Prestel in the United Kingdom and Minitel in France. Minitel, for instance, offers nearly free end user terminals to its subscribers along with a telephone directory look-up service (an electronic White Pages).

While videotex is not yet widely used in the U.S., many European countries have had government-run videotex services in place for some time now.

Both Prestel and Minitel use a packet network backbone to deliver videotex services to their subscribers, as do most other European providers of such services. Packet switched networks can also offer a partial solution to the problem of high terminal cost. An inexpensive asynchronous data terminal can access a wide variety of sophisticated interactive database services over a PSDN. In addition, their widespread deployment makes these networks ideally suited for reaching the mass market target for videotex. As the end user cost of videotex service decreases because of packet switching and innovative terminal distribution schemes, we will move closer to a true "electronic society."

DATABASE MEDIATION

The hundreds of information service providers in business in the U.S. today attest to the growing popularity of information retrieval from electronic databases. Unfortunately, each provider employs a different set of procedures to access and manipulate the data stored in the database. Log-on procedures vary widely, as do command and response formats, presenting difficulty for subscribers to multiple providers. In addition, subscribers to more than one provider often write down access and log-on charges, thereby creating a security problem. Database mediation provides a solution to these problems.

A database mediator is a host computer that performs translation between a user of multiple database services and the databases. A subscriber to a database mediation service first accesses the mediator host. This host presents a uniform, user-friendly interface (often a menu) that can be used to access and manipulate data from many different databases. The database mediator translates the end user commands into the specific format required by the database being accessed. It also translates responses from the database into a standard, user-friendly format. Using a database mediator, an end user can access and manipulate multiple databases with a single set of access, command and response procedures.

A database mediator enables a user to access and manipulate multiple databases with a single set of access, command, and response procedures.

Packet switching is the medium of choice for database mediation applications for several reasons. In today's marketplace, most information service providers deliver their database services through PSDNs such as Tymnet or Telenet. Thus the provider of a database mediator does not force a change in the service provider's basic data transport method. The cost-effectiveness of the PSDN is another major benefit in provision of database mediation. Finally, packet switching provides many additional features and benefits (widespread connectivity, short call setup delays, flexible billing options, optional user facilities) that make it attractive in database mediation applications.

PACKET SWITCHING AND ISDN

This is not the place to get into a lengthy discussion of what ISDN is. (If you're a little rusty on PRI, BRI, B channel, D channel, frame relay, and other ISDN nomenclature, you might want to check out Codex's *Basics Book of ISDN*.) To put it briefly, ISDN is an all digital network that provides various communications services (wideband and narrowband) through a standardized interface under end user control.

How does packet switching fit into ISDN? Essentially, it can play three roles:

- transporting signalling data on the D channel
- transporting end user data on the D channel
- transporting end user data on the B channel

(Procedures for exchanging end user data packets across the ISDN B and D channels are covered in CCITT Recommendation X.31.) The important thing to note here is that packet switching is compatible with—indeed, facilitates— migration to ISDN.

Access network (access layer)

The PADs and their associated user interfaces.

Address mapping

Establishes a virtual connection between two devices (usually, a terminal and a host application) by creating a temporary logical association between physical location and packet network addresses.

Backbone packet network (backbone layer)

The PNs and their associated internodal trunks.

Basic rate access interface

One of two interfaces available between ISDN end-users and the local ISDN exchange. The other is Primary rate access interface.

Call clearing packets

Disconnect a virtual circuit when the end-users no longer require the connection.

Call set-up packets

Establish a virtual circuit across a packet network.

Call clearing phase

The phase of a virtual connection during which both end-users receive an indication that they are no longer connected to each other.

Call set-up phase

The phase of a virtual connection during which the network nodes perform routing.

Communications subnetworks

Systems that support only the lowest three layers of the OSI model, providing transmission and networking.

Connectionless network

A packet network. (No physical wire connection implied.)

Connectivity

The ability of a device to communicate with other devices through a data communications facility.

Contention engineering

Conserves FEP resources by having the owner/operator of the host/FEP complex define only enough virtual terminals in the FEP to support the end-user terminals requiring simultaneous access to host applications during a busy period.

Data transfer phase

The phase of a virtual connection during which two end-users are in communication with each other, exchanging data.

Database mediator	A host computer that performs translation between a user of multiple database services and the databases.
Diagnostic packet	A special type of packet that performs network diagnostics.
Display System Protocol (DSP)	The transport protocol commonly used to carry a 3270 BSC data stream across an X.25 PSDN.
Drop	A terminal attachment to a multipoint line.
Echoplex	A manual error-control scheme
Emulation	The technique used by an HPAD to mimic the polling functions of the cluster controller/terminal.
Extended Logical Link Control (ELLC)	A variant of QLLC. See Qualified Logical Link Control.
External security	The ability of a data communications facility to protect the devices connected to it (terminals and host computers) from unwanted intrusion from the outside.
Frame	The unit of data transferred from one open system to another at OSI layer 2.
Hot-standby configuration	A PSDN node configuration in which the failure of a single node in a redundant pair does not cause an interruption of service through that node.
Internal security	The ability of a data communications facility to protect itself from unwanted intrusion from the outside.
Mesh configuration	A configuration of a PSDN in which more than one route may be selected to connect any two end users.
Mnemonic addressing	A process in which the 10-digit numeric addressing format used within the network is abbreviated to 3 or 4 alphanumeric characters to enhance the network's user-friendliness.
Negative acknowledgment (NAK)	A link control operation that causes retransmission of a frame.
Network address	A numerical identifier of a PSDN port.
Nodal buffer capacity	The capacity of the node to store end user data during overhead processing.

Optional Network Service Features	Attributes of a PSDN that affect the quality of service PSDN users can obtain.
OSI Model	Open Systems Interconnection model: specifies the characteristics of an open system.
Packet Assembler/Disassembler (PAD)	A device or program that allows end-user devices such as terminals to access a packet switched network.
Packet Switched Data Network (PSDN)	A network designed to carry data in the form of packets (see Packet switching).
Packet switching	A data networking technology in which user data is segmented into small units (packets) and sent from the sending user to the receiving user over shared communications channels.
Packet Switching Node (PN)	A termination point for two or more packet switched communication links. Its most important function is to ensure that each packet is routed to its proper destination.
Polling	A process in which an FEP sequentially polls the terminals connected to it, asking whether or not they have data to be sent to the host.
Positive acknowledgment (ACK)	A link control operation by which the receiver indicates to the sender that a data frame has been received without errors (causes sender to erase duplicate copy).
Primary rate access interface	One of two interfaces available between ISDN end-users and the local ISDN exchange. The other is Basic access interface.
Processing delay	The time taken by a PSDN to process and act upon the overhead information.
Protocol Transport	A process in which a PSDN carries data in one protocol (the native protocol) across the network by means of a second protocol (usually X.25 in public packet data networks).
Qualified Logical Link Control (QLLC)	The primary transport protocol used by X.25 packet networks to carry SNA data streams.

71

Reset packets	A packet type used by an X.25 PSDN to recover end-to-end virtual circuits after link layer failures.
Secondary channel	A side channel in the voice-frequency band used in modem diagnostic systems to transmit information about the state of the connection.
Signalling channel	The D channel of an ISDN interface.
Timesharing	A host computer process that runs interactive sessions with more than one operator terminal simultaneously.
Transmission delay	The delay resulting from the time taken by a packet to traverse an internodal trunk between two network nodes.
Transparency	The characteristic of a network to impose no restriction on the format and content of data it transports.
Value-added	A name given to some PSDNs because of the services provided by the host computers connected to them (example: E-mail).
Virtual circuit	A communications pathway between two users of a PSDN.
Virtual connection	The process by which end-users exchange data on a connectionless network (e.g., a PSDN).
Virtual terminals	A software image of a real terminal defined to the FEP at the time of network generation.
Window size	The number of frames that can be sent across a link before the sender must stop sending and wait for an acknowledgment from the receiver.
X.21bis	An alternative physical layer standard in X.25 to accommodate North American needs (equivalent to RS232C).

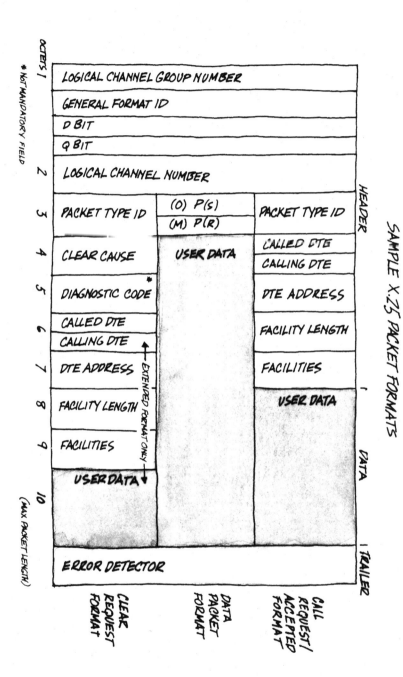

SAMPLE X-25 PACKET FORMATS

OCTETS			
1	LOGICAL CHANNEL GROUP NUMBER		
	GENERAL FORMAT ID		
	D BIT		
	Q BIT		
2	LOGICAL CHANNEL NUMBER		

*NOT MANDATORY FIELD

HEADER

3	PACKET TYPE ID	(O) P(s)	PACKET TYPE ID
		(M) P(R)	
4	CLEAR CAUSE	USER DATA	CALLED DTE
			CALLING DTE
5	DIAGNOSTIC CODE *		DTE ADDRESS
6	CALLED DTE		FACILITY LENGTH
	CALLING DTE		
7	DTE ADDRESS		FACILITIES
8	FACILITY LENGTH		USER DATA
9	FACILITIES		
10	USER DATA		

EXTENDED FORMAT ONLY

(MAX PACKET LENGTH)

DATA

ERROR DETECTOR

TRAILER

CLEAR REQUEST FORMAT   DATA PACKET FORMAT   CALL REQUEST/ ACCEPTED FORMAT

INDEX

I WANT TO KNOW MORE ABOUT MOTOROLA CODEX'S X.25 NETWORKING CAPABILITIES

☐ Please have a Motorola Codex representative call me.

My phone number is ( )_____

Best time to call: _____

☐ Please send me more information about Motorola Codex.

☐ Please send me information about other Motorola Codex products:

      ☐ Network management systems
      ☐ T1 and other digital products
      ☐ LAN internetworking products
      ☐ Modems
      ☐ Multiplexers
      ☐ ISDN

Name _____

Title _____

Company _____

Address _____

City_____ State_____ Zip_____

(Attach your business card here for faster processing.)